Did you just say
YOU STUPID
COMPUTER!

Did you just say YOU STUPID COMPUTER!

Tony Trombo
The Computer Guy

iUniverse, Inc.
New York Lincoln Shanghai

Did you just say YOU STUPID COMPUTER!

iUniverse, Inc.

For information address:
iUniverse, Inc.
2021 Pine Lake Road, Suite 100
Lincoln, NE 68512
www.iuniverse.com

ISBN: 0-595-30924-0

Printed in the United States of America

CONTENTS

NOTES

_____

_____

_____

_____

_____

_____

_____

_____

_____

_____

_____

_____

_____

_____

_____

_____

_____

_____

_____

_____

x / Did you just say YOU STUPID COMPUTER!

_____

_____

_____

_____

_____

_____

_____

_____

_____

_____

_____

_____

_____

_____

_____

_____

_____

_____

_____

_____

_____

_____

_____

_____

_____

_____

_____

NOTES

_____

_____

_____

_____

_____

_____

_____

_____

ABOUT THIS BOOK

I bought a computer book…once.

I thought that I'd get a few "tips and tricks" to help me along the path of computer wisdom.

Little did I know that under the fancy, colorful cover lied pages and pages of computer jargon that I had to lookup—in a separate computer dictionary—to figure out.

So what was the point of buying a SIMPLE TO UNDERSTAND computer book, when it took weeks to understand it!

When teaching computers, I quickly discovered that using the BIG computer words just was not going to cut it!

No, I had to really think about what I was saying, and how to explain it in such a way that someone who had never actually come in contact with a computer before purchasing one could follow my instructions.

The next thing I know, I'm out helping the next-door neighbors with their computer problems and questions!

The word quick spread that "some guy here in town" knows a lot about computers, and he's always willing and able to assist!

Things were getting out of hand! So I set up a website where people could email me questions. This turned out to be a good idea…for a while!

The poor old email box was getting filled up on a daily basis, and it was pretty much impossible to answer everybody.

I started keeping track of the questions, and I found that some would be asked over and over again. So my next brilliant move would be to publish the top 100 (or so) in a fancy, colorful book full of computer jargon…that you DON'T have to look up to understand!

Thus, this book was born! Not a lot of details. Just right-to-the-point answers to the best 100 computer questions that people me ask over and over again!

Remember, the information you're going to get in this book comes 100% from my experiences working with computers for many years. I put in my OPINIONS in with the facts. Things that I like may (or may not) be what you like. Working with computers is a personal thing. My goal is to help you have fun, and to get the benefits that your computer can offer!

Tony Trombo—the computer guy.

THE COMPUTER

Q: Why do they call it a MOUSE?

A: Here's the simple and straight forward answer: The little white thing (with a tail) that you hold to move the cursor around on the screen is called a MOUSE…because it looks like a MOUSE!

Really…I swear I didn't make that up!

Q: What is a CURSOR?

A: When you move your mouse, the thing that moves on the screen is called the CURSOR. I sometimes call it the Pointer. It's up to you how you want to refer to it!

Q: I only use the LEFT MOUSE BUTTON. What is the RIGHT one for?

A: Let's say that you're on a web page. When you click on something, the Left mouse button MAKES IT do what it's supposed to do.

Sometimes clicking on an object takes you to a web page. Sometimes it starts a video. Sometimes it plays a sound. There are many things Left clicking can do.

Clicking on an object with the Right Button shows you the variations on WHAT it can do.

I always say, "Left click on everything! See what happens! See where it takes you!" I guess while you're at it, you should Right click on things too. You'll quickly learn what things can and can't do!

Q: I keep reading about the QWERT keyboard. What is that?

A: If you're in the United States (and other Western countries) the QWERT is the keyboard that you have. The first 6 letters on the top row of the left hand side just happen to be Q W E R T Y.

I was in France a few years ago when I made an amazing discovery…their keyboards have only SOME of the keys in the same place! It wasn't even that really noticeable until I typed (without looking at the keyboard) "Hello how are you." And it came out "Hqllpw hwk are ywu?"

Q: What are those "F" buttons on the top of my keyboard?

A: Those buttons are used as SHORTCUTS. They'll get you to different pages. For example, the F1 Key usually opens up the HELP window. You'll find that some of them don't seem to do anything! Some programs that you buy will make good use of all of them. The buttons are ASSIGNABLE so they change their duties as needed.

Q: What is the button labeled CTRL?

A: That's the CONTROL KEY. When you hold it down and (at the same time) hit another key, it tells the computer you want to do something. That "something" could be just about anything, depending on the program that you are working with.

For example, holding down CONTROL and the "P" key usually PRINTS the page you have in front of you.

Holding down CONTROL and the "S" KEY will usually SAVE what you're working on.

These are called KEYBOARD SHORTCUTS. When you get used to using them, it can save you a lot of time!

Q: What is the ALT button?

A: That little guy is the ALTERNATE button. It works very much like the CONTROL KEY.

Q: What does the ESC button do?

A: The ESCAPE button almost like a panic button! When things take too long, or you want to stop what's happening, you can sometimes hit the ESCAPE button to stop it.

I'm glad the ESCAPE button is there, but more often then not, it doesn't do much of anything! Give it a try when you think need it, but don't hold your breath! It won't hurt anything to hit it, so you don't have anything to lose!

Q: Why do they call it the DESKTOP?

A: You should think of your computer as a DESK. You can put things into it, and it's a good place to get a lot of work done. The main screen that you see when all the programs are closed is called the DESKTOP.

Q: What is a TASKBAR?

A: The TASKBAR is the located at the VERY BOTTOM of the DESKTOP on your screen. You should see the START BUTTON on the far left of the TASKBAR. You may see the CLOCK on the far right.

When you start a program, the name of the program appears on the TASKBAR. This lets you know that the program is open and running.

Q: What is a WINDOW?

A: Programs will open up in a WINDOW. This WINDOW sits on top of your desktop. Sometimes is covers the entire desktop, or sometimes it's smaller and allows you to see the desktop underneath it.

You can change the size of the WINDOW in a few different ways.

On the top right hand side of a WINDOW, you'll see three little boxes. One has a MINUS SIGN, next is a BOX, and next is an X.

If you 1) LEFT CLICK on the MINUS SIGN, the WINDOW shrinks up and goes down on the TASKBAR on the bottom of the screen. This means that the program is still open and running, it's now just MINIMIZED to get it out of the way while you work on something else!

You can also 2) CLICK on the BOX on the WIN-DOW. One click and the window covers the entire desktop. Another click and the window gets smaller. It's your choice on what size you want the window to be. It makes no difference to the program or how it runs.

You can also 3) click on the X button. This completely shuts down the WINDOW and closes the program. Make sure you have all your work SAVED before hitting the X button!

Q: How do I move the WINDOW out of the way?

A: You can move the WINDOW around on the screen, and put it where you want it! Just click and HOLD the left mouse button on the TOP of the WINDOW. You can then DRAG the WIN-DOW around on the screen! When you let go of the mouse button, it drops the WINDOW right there. You'll use this feature a lot, so I suggest that you give it a try now!

You can also change the SHAPE of the WIN-DOW by left clicking on any EDGE and (while holding down the left mouse button) dragging the window into different sizes!

Q: Can I have more than one WINDOW open at once?

A: You can have many, many WINDOWS open at the same time. Each WINDOW can have a different program running, or sometimes one program can have a need for many WINDOWS to be open. It just depends of how you're using the computer at the time.

Q: What is MULTI-TASKING?

A: Running more than one program at a time is known as MULTI-TASKING. You can be writing a letter with one program, making a Christmas card with another program, and at the same time searching the Internet…jumping from one program to another at will!

There's no need to shut off one program before starting another one (like in the "old days" of computers!)

Q: What is MAXIMIXE and MINIMIZE?

A; Like we were talking about a few seconds ago, hitting the MINUS button on the right hand side of a window will MINIMIZE it down to the taskbar, where it will still be running, just out of your way.

If the window is MIMNIMIZED, you can click on it while it sits on the taskbar to bring it back up to the desktop.

Q: What is DRAG AND DROP?

A: DRAG and DROP is what we talked about a few moments ago. You can left click on something (while holding the mouse button down) and DRAG the thing to a new location and DROP it there by letting go of the mouse button. Our previous example was a window, but you can use it for many other things! It's good to experiment with DRAG and DROP a few times to get the hang of it! It's VERY useful for many programs!

Q: How do you COPY AND PASTE, and what do you use it for?

A: COPY and PASTE is one of those neat features that can save you hours of time and effort!

Lets say that you have found a paragraph on the Internet that you want to use in a report. You COULD sit there and re-type it all...or you could just COPY and PASTE it into your report in a few seconds!

First, you need to HIGHLIGHT the words you want to COPY to your report. HIGHLIGHTING is telling the computer exactly WHAT words you want to COPY.

To HIGHLIGHT a paragraph, you simply put your CURSOR just to the left of the first word in the sentence.

You hold down the LEFT mouse button and drag the CURSOR across the rest of the sentence (or the entire paragraph if you wish.) The letters will reverse color (instead of black letters on white paper, they'll be white letters on black paper.)

We have just told the computer that those are the words we want to COPY!

Now you RIGHT CLICK on the words you just HIGHLIGHTED. The computer will ask you what you want to do with those highlighted words. Select COPY from the list.

The highlighted words are now COPIED on the CLIPBOARD. The clipboard is an invisible window that holds what you just copied until you need to use it later. You may not need to PASTE the sentence that you just COPIED for a few minutes (or a few hours), so they'll sit and wait for you, safe on the CLIPBOARD!

If you open up your typing program such a WINDOWS NOTEBOOK or MICROSOFT WORD (if you have it on your computer), you can now PASTE the sentence from the CLIP-BOARD to your new document!

RIGHT CLICK on the new document and select the PASTE option.

You'll see the very sentence that you previously COPIED to the CLIPBOARD is now on your new document…exactly like the original!

You can COPY and PASTE words AND pictures to the clipboard to use in your documents! The only bad thing about the CLIPBOARD is that you can only COPY one thing at a time! The previously copied items are always erased when you copy something new to the clipboard…so be careful!

There is also another term called CUT and PASTE. It acts pretty much the same as COPY and PASTE except the original text (words) will disappear from the original document when you CUT them to the clipboard. The COPY command leaves them alone.

Q: What is an ICON?

A: Back in the old days of computers, you had to type in line after line after line of computer commands to make your machine work!

Now days you just click on a little colorful picture on the desktop (called an ICON) that makes the computer do what you want it to do! Normally, programs don't sit on the desktop, but an ICON representing the program takes you there instead. It's called a shortcut…

Q: What is a SHORTCUT?

A: A SHORTCUT starts a program in your computer…usually from the desktop.

When you install a program in your computer, it goes deep inside and could take a few minutes of searching for you to find it to use it. Luckily, most programs will put a shortcut ICON on the desktop for you.

If not, you can always find a shortcut to your programs by click the START button (on the lower left hand corner of the screen), and clicking on PROGRAMS. There you'll see most everything you need to use in the computer.

Q: I found something that says "MY COMPUTER" What is it?

A: When you want to see totally everything that's in your computer, you'll click on MY COMPUTER. You may or may not want to know! It's up to you! Don't worry about "breaking" anything. If you dig around and get into places where you shouldn't be, the computer will start popping up warnings for you to stop!

Q: I looked in MY COMPUTER, and I see different things like the A DRIVE, the C DRIVE? What does that mean?

A: Remembering that your computer is like a desk, a desk has drawers (or DRIVES) to keep thing in.

Most computers have a couple of places to keep your programs, pictures, documents and music. These act as drawers (also called FOLDERS) in the DRIVES for your stuff.

The one that you use mostly is called the C DRIVE. Unless you actually take the screws off of the back of the computer and look inside, you'll never see the physical C DRIVE!

Because the computer knows that you can store MANY different types of things in it, it allows you to DIVIDE it up into sections (FOLDERS) to keep thing organized!

Your computer comes with several folders already in its C DRIVE when you buy it! One is called MY DOCUMENTS. In MY DOCUMENTS you'll find sever smaller folders for even better organizing of your stuff!

One of the smaller folders is called MY MUSIC. One is called MY PICTURES. Each folder can hold an almost unlimited amount of items!

The A DRIVE is the FLOPPY DISK. I'll explain what that is a little later in the book

The CD ROM (or CD player) is sometimes called the D DRIVE.

Q: I have read that you can never have enough RAM, but I don't know what it is!

A: Without going into a lot details, RAM stands for Random Access Memory. It's like computer brainpower! The more RAM you have, the faster and more efficient the computer is!

RAM comes in chips that you buy at the computer store. You computer came with some, but there's most always room in there for more!

Most computers come with about 128 MEGABYTES (a unit of measurement) of RAM. As of this printing (2004), you can buy a 128-megabyte chip for about $45. If this is a 3-year-old book, that same amount of RAM is probably down to about $1!

The price drops like a rock on computer stuff!

Q: Is the CD ROM in my computer like a regular CD player?

A: Yep! It can play your CDs! And if you're hooked to the Internet, the computer can tell you the name of each song, who the artist is, and give you a complete biography of the band!

Ain't technology Fun?!

Q: Can I make my own CDs?

A: Yes, if your CD ROM is a CD burner. You can buy songs on the Internet and put (burn) them onto a blank CD to play in your other CD players!

Ain't technology fun (again)!

Q: Can I make my own DVDs?

A: Now the whole DVD burning thing gets a little trickier.

If your computer doesn't have a VIDEO CAPTURE CARD on it, you'll need to buy one. A VIDEO CAPTURE CARD grabs the video from your VCR and puts it into the computer. It's called ANALOGUE to DIGITAL CONVERSION.

The trouble is that the computer can COMPRESS the video so it works better on your computer. COMPRESSING video really can take away the quality.

The Video Capture Card that you buy will tell you if it will compress the incoming video or not. It's really easy to tell without even looking…if it's a

$99 Video Capture Card; it's going to compress the video!

If it's a $700 Video Capture Card, it'll capture the video with any noticeable loss of quality. If you want to take a VHS tape and burn it exactly to a DVD…you'll need the $700 Capture Card.

Some Digital Camcorders will have an Analogue to Digital converter built in, so you may save yourself a bit-o-money there.

You'll also need some DVD burning software. There's good and bad in that lot too!

Sometimes it's just better to take the VHS tape down to a local drugstore that offers the DVD transfer service for $25…and have them do it for you!

Q: Can I hurt my computer by clicking on things?

A: Nope! Click on EVERYTHING! The more you click, the more you learn!

If you get near something in the computer that you SHOULD NOT be clicking on, it'll warn you to stop!

Q: What if my computer won't come on?

A: You're doomed!

Okay…"Doomed" might be the wrong word! Check to see if the computer is plugged in. Next, check to see that the monitor is plugged in and turned on.

If all else fails, take it into the local computer repair shop.

I sure wish I had a better answer, but a dead computer is hard to fix unless you really know what you're doing!

Sometimes it's cheaper just to go out and buy a new computer…you'll find out…

Q: My friend says that I shouldn't hit the RESET BUTTON. Is that true?

A: Yea, the evil RESET BUTTON on the front of the computer shouldn't be used unless it's absolutely necessary.

Sometimes the computer just totally freezes up and the ONLY way to get it "unstuck" is to use the RESET button to shut it down and restart Windows.

I've messed up my computer BAD using the reset button!

…And NEVER unplug the computer while it's on!

To shut down the computer you should ALWAYS go to the START BUTTON and click on SHUT DOWN.

My professional advice is to NEVER EVER shut the computer off unless you're going on vacation for longer that 3 or 4 days. The computer LIKES to be on all the time. It works better and the programs are less likely to get "problems"!

I WOULD shut the monitor off when you're not using it. Your electricity bill will thank you too!

Q: I have never used my FLOPPY DISK. Why is it there?

A: The old faithful FLOPPY DISK was the only way to save things a few years ago! Now it's just a stupid old, out of date thing that should not be!

But (unlike other parts) the FLOPPY DISK almost always works, regardless of how messed up your computer might get!

So, in case of emergency you can make a START UP DISK (at least in Windows ME) to get your computer started when all else fails.

Q: I like to play games on the computer, but it seems to run slower and slower each time I add another game. Why?

A: I hate computer games.

Don't get me wrong; games on an X BOX are the coolest things ever. Just leave the games for the game consoles and keep 'um off the computer (in my opinion.)

Games put a tremendous amount of strain on the computer (unless you've got the fastest computer going), and the more you dump into the computer the worse off it'll be.

If you disagree…fine.

But I'm right!

Q: What is DEFRAGMENTING?

A: Every time that you put in (or take out) a program it can FRAGMENT the other programs on the hard drive.

Little bits of program information gets scattered, and that makes it that much harder for the computer to find all the little pieces to run the programs.

DEFRAGMENTING takes a while, but the computer looks over everything in its body and reassembles the programs so it works more efficiently.

You DEFRAGMENT your computer differently depending on which version of Windows you have (98, ME, 200, XP). Hit the F1 button and type in DEFRAGMENT to find out how to do this little trick.

Q: Why should I buy a BATTERY BACKUP?

A: When the power goes out, your computer shuts off, and like I said before, it just isn't good!

A BATTERY BACKUP will keep the computer on (for a short while) when the lights go off in a storm!

Q: What is a POWER SERGE PROTECTOR?

A: Let's take that same storm…lighting strikes near the house and a serge of electricity comes down the line and into your computer.

Kentucky Fried Computer (KFC)!

Go right out and buy SERGE PROTECTORS for your computer and your TVs!

Q: What is an UPGRADE?

A: You bought your computer with a copy of Windows (the operating system). Maybe you have Windows ME...now it's time to UPGRADE to Windows XP!

You should try and have the latest version of Windows. Programs are written assuming that you're current with you operating systems. It costs a lot, and I don't like it a bit...but what can ya do?!

Q: What does it mean to UPDATE WINDOWS?

A: Windows offers FREE updates (not upgrades...but updates) to its operating systems from time to time. When you go on the Internet, Microsoft will let you know when an update is available. They'll send it to you over the Internet.

Q: What does 5.1 mean?

If you've got a DVD player (not the one in your computer...the one in the stereo rack), and it's hooked up to 2 speakers, that's called STEREO sound. When you get into the 6 speaker systems, that's a 5.1 system (5 speakers and 1 big 'old sub-woofer to shake the paintings off the wall!)

Sometimes a computer has a soundcard that will play your DVDs in 5.1 sound when properly hooded up to a proper receiver.

Q: What is a SOUNDCARD?

A: The computer makes all those cool (or annoying) sounds. But the actual "computer" doesn't make much more sounds that a simple BEEP from a tiny speaker in the case.

No…the sounds really come from a little device in the computer's case called the SOUND CARD.

There are many different kinds of sound cards. Some are better than others. Some do more than others.

They all are designed to produce sounds. Sounds from your CDs, DVDs or the computer's sounds.

Q: I have WINDOWS MEDIA PLAYER on my computer. What all does it do?

A: WINDOWS MEDIA PLAYER is like a jukebox for your computer. It will control your CD player, and if you're hooked to the Internet, WMP will tell you what songs are on the CD, the Artists information and (sometimes) pictures and video from the album!

You can also search the planet for radio stations to listen to. I've even found police and air traffic signals from most of the major cities in the U.S.!

If you play around with WMP, you'll find really cool stuff that will keep you busy for hours!

Q: Sometimes the computer says that I need to download and install FLASH. What is it?

A: FLASH is a program that allows websites to have really fantastic presentations (or even cartoon type movies) displayed on your computer.

You can't see a Flash movie unless you have the Flash player installed on your computer. If you agree to install Flash, you're taken to a website where you can get the player for free!

Q: What is REAL PLAYER?

A: WINDOWS MEDIA PLAYER comes with Windows in your computer. But it's not the only game in the Internet town!

REAL PLAYER is a music and video player too. Some websites have music or video that can only been seen with REAL PLAYER, so you may get a message saying that you need it. They'll send you to the correct website to get it.

Q: What is QUICKTIME?

A: QuickTime is yet another way you may listen to music and video. You may find that you need it when visiting a website. You know the drill…

Q: What is a DRIVER?

A: When you buy a new part (say…a printer) for your computer, your computer needs to know what it is, and how it works.

A disk comes with your new printer that gives the computer this information.

This information is called the DRIVER.

Sometimes this DRIVER gets messed up the computer's brain (don't ask me how) and needs to be re-installed. So don't lose the disk, you may need it later.

Q: Do I need a BIGGER MONITOR?

A: Yes, Always YES (unless you've got some huge 21 inch monster monitor!) The larger the screen, the more stuff you can see and the bigger the stuff on the screen can be!

Q: My friend has 2 MONITORS on his computer. What is the advantage?

A: Sometimes programs have so much stuff they need to show you on the screen that they suggest that you have TWO MONITORS.

I wouldn't go so far as to get more than one monitor if you don't absolutely need it. It's just one more thin to worry about (I have 3…by the way.)

Q: What is the OPERATING SYSTEM?

A: WINDOWS is an OPERATING SYSTEM. You work the computer with the operating system. Instead of typing a zillion lines of "computer lingo", you just click on things on the screen and the OPERATING SYSTEM does the work for you!

Q: Why do I need to use a SCREEN SAVER?

A: When you leave your computer for the night without shutting off the monitor, whatever is in the screen can "Burn" its image permanently on the monitor.

It may not happen overnight, but if you do it long enough, you'll start to see the faint image on the screen.

This is not a good thing!

A SCREEN SAVER is a little program that comes on if you don't touch the computer for a certain amount of time. The screen goes blank for a second and then an image comes on that moves around, keeping the screen from getting ruined.

Q: How long should my computer last?

A: They say (who ever "they" are…) that computers double in speed every 18 months, making the one the YOU have old and out-of-date!

This may or may not be true.

Yea, they pretty much DO double in speed every 18 months, but there may not be a real NEED for you to run right out and buy a brand new computer!

I've been told that the HARD DRIVE (the device in your computer where your programs and data are stored) will last about 5 years before it's time to get a replacement.

Most humans don't need anywhere CLOSE to the power and speed of the "top end" home computer. I wouldn't buy another one until you go over to your friend's house…and use theirs.

Then the trouble begins!

When you see that THEIR computer goes from Shut Down to Fully Up And Running 10 times faster than your dumb old wreck of a computer, then (simply out of jealousy) should you go and drop another $1500 at Bob's Computer and Kitchen Appliances World!

Maybe keeping up with the Jones' IS important after all!

Q: What is the START BUTTON for?

A: The START BUTTON is a nice touch for the new computer user. Whenever you need to find your programs, or change things in the computer, you can always click on START!

Like everything else in the computer, there's about 10 different ways to do ANYTHING you need to do. Going to the START BUTTON in one of them, and makes your computer life easier!

Q: I wrote a letter and saved it, but now I can't seem to find it on the computer! How can I get it back?

A: Ah yes, the old 'the computer ate my letter" trick!

WINDOWS has a really cool feature that I use all the time…it's called SEARCH. You just type in the name (or part of the name) of the file you're looking for, and the computer finds it for you!

In other words, if you named your lost letter "LETTER TO MOM", you can type in "MOM", and every file in the computer with the word "MOM" in it will come up on a list in front of you.

You can then find your missing letter, open it and save it where you'll remember where it is next time!

Normally you can do a search by clicking on the START BUTTON (Lower left hand side of the screen) and you'll see SEARCH. Click on it, and it'll walk you through the easy process of finding what you lost!

Q: My computer came with NOTEPAD for writing letters. Do I need to buy another program?

A: NOTEPAD is a very simple little program that allows you to write and print letters. It doesn't have much in the way of EDITING.

I'm the worst typist in the world, so I need all the help I can get from my typing program! I live for the SPELL CHECKER!

I use Microsoft Word. I'm not saying that it's the best or the worst…but I bought it, and I know how to use it fairly well. You should just go to the computer store and check out all the different companies that make this type of software. It'll really come down to how much you want to spend!

Q: Should I get a LAPTOP computer instead of a DESKTOP computer?

A: Are you going somewhere that you need to take your computer? Yes if yes. No if no.

Desktop computers cost a lot less money! The monitor screen is (usually) bigger and easier to read. You can open up a desktop computer and install new stuff inside easier.

Don't get me wrong, I really like my Laptop...but I drag the thing around with me quite a bit. I say start with a desktop computer, and buy a Laptop later IF you feel you need one.

Q: Did MICROSOFT invent the computer?

A: His name was Billy Wayne Microsoft from Lexington, Kentucky. In 1894 his invented the computer, which at that time was nothing more than two pieces of metal tied to a...

Oh, heck...ya caught me!

No. Microsoft and Bill Gates DIDN'T invent the computer.

He DID invent the little thing called WINDOWS that works in the computer! It made the computer easier to use for the "regular folks" like you and me!

It also made him a BAZILLIONARE by selling tons of copies (and all the subsequent versions) of Windows to most everyone on the planet who owns a Personal Computer (PC).

Q: What is a NETWORK?

A: More that one computer working together.

Q: Do I need a NETWORK at home?

A: Home NETWORKING has a lot of advantages.

Back in the old days when there was only ONE computer per house, NETWORKING really didn't apply.

Now that a lot of houses have several computers, NETWORKING can actually save you money by SHARING things like printers and scanners.

Lets say that your computer is upstairs, and the kid's computer(s) are down in their rooms. You own the family printer, and it's upstairs with you.

NETWORKING allows the kids to print documents from their computers on YOUR printer. One printer works for all the computers in the house! NICE!

The disadvantage is that when they want to get their nice printed document, they have to run all the way upstairs to get it! Also, the poor old printer also gets used a lot more, and its INK gets used up faster!

Networking can be done with WIRES (that you run all through the house) or WIRELESS by using small transmitters and receivers on the computers. I like NETWORKING, but it's not for everyone.

NOTES

_____

_____

_____

_____

_____

_____

_____

_____

_____

_____

_____

_____

_____

_____

_____

_____

_____

_____

_____

_____

_____

_____

_____

_____

_____

_____

_____

_____

_____

_____

_____

_____

_____

_____

_____

_____

_____

_____

_____

_____

_____

_____

_____

_____

_____

_____

_____

_____

_____

_____

_____

_____

_____

_____

_____

_____

_____

_____

_____

_____

_____

_____

_____

_____

_____

_____

_____

_____

_____

_____

_____

_____

_____

THE INTERNET

Q: What is the INTERNET?

A: The INTERNET is millions and millions of computers hooked together to form one big, World Wide thing.

Q: What can I do with it?

A: When you're on the Internet, you can find out about almost ANY subject, buy almost ANY product, and communicate with people like you were right there with them, even if they're 10,000 miles away!

Q: Do people watch what you're doing while your on the INTERNET?

A: Nope. That's the great thing about the Internet; you're free to do what you want.

That been said, if you try something ILLEGAL on the Internet, the Government CAN track you down (with almost no trouble at all!), so don't be stupid!

People think that they have total privacy on the Internet. Not exactly true!

Q: Who can I trust on the INTERNET?

A: Really...I wouldn't actually TRUST anybody on the Internet unless it's a Major Company that you can do some research on first.

I mean if you buy something from www.WAL-MART.com...you're safe enough! But companies you don't know may be a different story. Use your best judgment!

Also, there are CHATROOMS where you can meet and talk (type) to people that share your interest. They can be really fun and you can have a great time…BUT you have to remember that you really don't have ANY IDEA who you're talking to! Just because he SAYS he's hansom and 23 from Houston and drives a red sports car to multi-million dollar estate, COULD just mean that he's 57, ugly, stupid and in PRISION for murder in Maine!

Be careful!

Q: What is a WEBSITE?

A: A WEBSITE is a page much like a page in a newspaper. It has words and pictures and colors, and sometimes music and video.

When you go on the Internet, you're looking at WEBSITES!

Q: I have a small business. I'd like to have a WEB-SITE of my own. How do I go about getting one?

A: You can hire a WEBMASTER to make one for you. You can find many of them in the Yellow

Pages or in the newspaper. They charge a fee to get your site up and running. They will also maintain the site for you if you want any changes made later.

You can also buy a WEB SITE BUILDING program at the computer store. Most of them are relatively easy to work with (if you're at all good with art), and you can take all the time you need to make it EXACTLY how you want!

Once your website is done and looking the way you want, you'll need to find a HOST so that the rest of the planet can see what you have to offer.

A lot of companies sell WEB SPACE for a small amount of money per month. Your website gets transferred to them, and it becomes available to the public.

Q: I'd like to have my own WEB ADDRESS. How do I get one?

A: I have www.YouStupidComputer.biz (along with a bunch of others) that I RENT on a yearly basis from a company called www.GoDaddy.com for about $9.

I made my own website, found a company to host it, and I FORWARD people to my site when they type in my WEB ADDRESS on their computers.

The whole process is relative simple, and once it's done...it's done for good...but I suggest that you hire somebody to help you on your first website.

Q: How many email addresses can I have?

A: Unlimited. As long as the email address names you want are available!

Q: Can I read my email from any computer, or just mine at home?

A: You can most always access your email from any computer on the PLANET! There might be an exception here and there depending on what company you have your email service with, but 99% of the time you're free to travel and keep up with your family and friend's letters!

In some places, you can access your computer from special Public Telephones that have a computer screen attached.

Q: Can anyone else read my email?

A: Not unless you give them your PASSWORD to get into your email account.

Q: What does it mean to FORWARD an email?

A: If you get an email, you can FORWARD it to another email address. This sends a copy of the original email to someone else that you think might like to read it.

Q: What is a REPLY to an email?

A: If someone sends you an email, you can REPLY to him or her. You call it "writing back".

Q: What is UPLOADING?

A: You can send pictures in an email. The computer UPLOADS the picture from your computer and sends it to whomever you're emailing as an ATTACHMENT. An ATTACHMENT is something that goes along with your email. It can be a picture, some music, or a program.

Q: What is DOWNLOADING?

A: When you GET an email with a picture attached, you DOWNLOAD it into your computer.

You must be VERY careful what you download into your computer. I highly suggest that you NEVER download anything from an email into your computer unless you are absolutely positive who it came from! You could get a very nasty VIRUS!

Q: What is a VIRUS?

A: A VIRUS is usually sent to you through an email as an Attachment. When you open the

Attachment, it can turn out to be a destructive little program that can do an unlimited amount of damage to your poor computer!

You're safe to READ your email, but if you don't know who sent the Attachment that came with it…don't download and/or open it!

Q: How can I protect myself from getting a VIRUS?

A: There are a number of ANTI-VIRUS software packages that you can buy at the store. They are kept up-to-date to counteract and fix (or stop) the latest and nastiest viruses that jump into your computer.

YOU MUST GET AN ANTI-VIRUS PROGRAM!

Q: What is a FIREWALL?

A: A FIREWALL is a little program that watches what comes in and goes out of your computer. If somebody tries to HACK into your computer, it SHOULD stop him or her.

I feel better about having a FIREWALL on my computer. You should look into getting one just to be on the safe side.

Q: How much does it cost to email my brother in England?

A: The great thing about the World Wide Web is that you can send an email NEXT DOOR for free…and then send an email overseas for the same LOW PRICE (of FREE)…and just as fast too!

Q: How long does email take to get to where I send it?

A: Usually only a second or two. ZOOM!

Q: What is DIAL UP?

A: When you get your Internet Service by using the regular Telephone Line, that's DIAL UP. It's really slow and horrible, and should be outlawed!

Q: What is a CABLE MODEM?

A: That's when you get your Internet from the Cable Company using your Cable TV wires. Now we're talking about SPEED!

Q: What is DSL?

A: DSL is the getting the Internet using your Telephone Line, but using a DIGITAL SIGNAL. It makes it really fast, and doesn't tie up your Telephone lines!

Q: How do I buy something from the INTER-NET?

A: You can go to an Internet AUCTION or use a SHOPPING service. I'll explain in a minute...

Q: How do I PAY for what I buy?

A: If you buy something on the Internet, you can send the company (or person) a Check, a Money Order, or use your Credit Card.

Q: Is giving my CREDIT CARD NUMBER over the Internet safe?

A: It depends on whom you're dealing with! I don't mind giving my card number out to a BIG company (like a Walmart or Sears), but anyone else is getting paid some other way.

Q: Is there a safe way to buy things on line?

A: Use a pay service, such as PAYPAL.

Q: What is PAYPAL?

A: I give my Credit Card Number to the good people at www.PAYPAL.com. When I buy something, PAYPAL sends them the money for me. My card number NEVER gets in the hands of the Seller!

There are also some other services like www. PAYDIRECT.com who do the same thing.

The only trouble is that not everyone TAKES Paypal or Paydirect for purchases. You have to decide if you feel comfortable with giving the seller your Credit Card Number.

If not, don't buy from them!

Q: What is an ON LINE AUCTION?

A: An ON LINE AUCTION (such a www. EBAY.com) is a fantastic way to find almost ANYTHING you're looking to buy! It's kind of like the worlds largest garage sale with MIL-LIONS of products for sale, 24 hours a day!

There are many other auction sites on the Internet, but Ebay is the biggest, and my personal favorite.

You just find what you're looking for, bid on it, and wait to see what happens! I get all kinds of stuff (that I may or may not really need) from auctions.

You'll find stupid stuff that cost $0.01…to Multi Million dollar homes listed for bidding! It's WAY more fun than should be legal!

Q: What is YAHOO?

A: YAHOO is a company that offers News, Sports, Weather, Email, Shopping and about 5 zillion other services for free!

I like YAHOO because it's pretty easy to use and you can find the KILLER shopping deals there!

Q: Can I just SHOP on line without going into an auction?

A: Sure! www.SHOP.com is just one of MANY, MANY places to buy stuff on the Internet! YAHOO has a fantastic Shopping section. If you can't find a deal on something there, you're just not looking hard enough!

Q: Can I compare prices from several different stores before I make a decision?

A: Most places like YAHOO or MSN will let you shop and compare prices from MANY different stores. It's like having 100 catalogues in front of you, and seeing who has the best deal!

FUN, FUN, FUN!

Q: What is a HOMEPAGE?

A: When you click on the little blue "E" (on a PC) to start Internet Explorer, the first page you go to is called your HOME PAGE.

Q: Why do I sometimes need a PASSWORD?

A: A password protects you from other people accessing your stuff!

You need a password to get into certain websites, or to check your email. I TRY and use the same password for everything I do, but that always doesn't work out, so I keep a little file box next to the desk to write them down in case I forget.

Q: I get a lot of email from people I don't even know! How do I stop it?

A: That's called SPAM...and I hate it! But there's not a lot you can do about it. There are FILTERS that you can get to send unwanted email to a special "SPAM" folder for you to delete later, but they only work SO WELL!

Q: If I change my email address, can I have my email forwarded to my new address?

A: Normally…no. That's the bad part about getting 10,000 UNWANTED spam emails in your IN BOX per day, and deciding to just GIVE UP on your old email address and get a brand new one…that the advertisers don't know about (yet).

You have to tell all your friends and family your new email address so they can fine you again!

Q: What are EMOTIONS in my email?

A: The little yellow HAPPY FACE guy can be inserted in your email (if offered by whoever your email account is with) to show EMOTIONS.

Sometimes he's Happy.

Sometimes he's Sad.

Sometimes he's Mad.

Sometimes he's really stupid and annoying and I wish he's just get off of my email!

I guess I need a MAD Happy Face Guy right about now!

Q: My email looks dull. Can I add colors and pictures to it?

A: Most Internet Service Providers (ISPs), AOL for example, give you the options of adding all kind of cool looking stuff you're your email! There are programs that you can buy to add things too if your ISP doesn't offer it.

Q: What is HTML?

A: Hyper Text Markup Language. Computer lingo!

A web page is not REALLY a page, but a lot of PARTS (pictures, colors, text and/or sounds) put together to form a website.

People use HTML to tell the computer "what and where" these part go on your screen to make the page that you see.

Making a website used to require you to know HTML. Now you can buy programs that make it a lot simpler!

Q: Is on-line GAMBLING legal?

A: Gambling on the Internet would be illegal, but because it's WORLD WIDE, you're probably actually sending your money OFF SHORE (to another country) where it's "Okay".

Vegas gives out some pretty good odds, just to get you there. You odds of winning on the Internet are (shall we say) LESS!

Tell you what…if you really want to gamble on the Internet, how about this: Pick a number between 1 and 1000. Done?

If I don't guess it correctly, you send me all your money!

My answer is 24.

Wrong?

Excellent! Just make that check payable to the California Advisory System Hierarchy (C.A.S.H.) and send it right to me.

Thank you!

Q: There are so many websites…how do I find the one that I'm looking for?

A: Search for it.

Q: What is an INTERNET SEARCH?

A: The Internet is a HUGE place! You'll probably find a box on the top of the screen when you're on the Internet that says "SEARCH". Type in what you are looking for, and it'll find you websites that correspond to your KEYWORDS!

Q: What is a KEYWORD?

A: When you do a search for something, you use KEYWORDS. I like to use www.Google.com for my search engine. When I'm there, I don't have to type in "Please show me a website about Alaskan Brown Bears". I just type in a few KEYWORDS like "Alaskan Brown Bear" and I get 40,700 websites to chose from.

The more keywords you use in a search, the more it will narrow down your search. If I didn't type in "Brown" in the previous example, Google gives me 137,000 sites to choose from!

Q: Why do I get so many ADS for products while I'm on the Internet?

A: Everybody has something to sell on the Internet! If you have a website that gets a lot of people looking at it (traffic), you too can sell ads!

I don't understand why we must PAY for the Internet, when we're bombarded with ads while we're using it! I would think that big companies like AOL would lets us use the Internet for FREE just to get more people looking at their ads.

Oh well, I guess I pay for the Newspaper, and it's full of ads too!

Q: What is a POP UP AD?

A: Pop up ads were most likely invented by SATIN to torture and torment all who come in contact with them!

You'll be having a wonderful time, searching the Internet, when BAM! The stupid POP UP AD…pops up in front of you! It's designed to get your attention, and it DOES do a good job of that!

Unfortunately for all of us, we rarely ever want to BUY the dumb product that's they're pushing in our faces!

You can buy a little program called a POP UP STOPPER, (or BLOCKER) which will shut the pop up ads down before they ever reach your eyes!

Q: I tried to look at a website from China. The computer told me I needed to download the CHARACTERS to make the page work correctly. What does that mean?

A: When you're trying to see a website from a country that uses text other than standard English, the computer will ask you if you want to download the new characters. If you say YES, it takes a few moments, and the computer will send you on your way to the site when it's done installing the new FONTS (called Characters or Text).

Q: What is a TOOL BAR?

A: The TOOL BAR is located at the top of the screen when you're on the Internet. Usually, there are a few choices like FILE, EDIT, VIEW, FAVORITES, TOOLS and HELP.

Some companies like YAHOO and EBAY offer their own free TOOLS BARS to help you take advantage of their websites. You can download these handy things from them!

Q: Sometimes I try to get on the Internet and I get a very strange white page that says it's not available. Is there a certain time of day that the Internet doesn't work?

A: Nope. The Internet works 24/7/365. It never sleeps, eats, or takes a break for lunch! Considering that the World Wide Web is…well…world wide, there's always millions and millions of people using it all the time!

Q: Who owns the Internet?

A: Al Gore, the inventor of the Internet…and me. We split the profits 50/50.

Really…nobody owns it. Some people just make more MONEY from it than others!

Q: What is a BOOKMARK?

A: When you visit a website, it's sometimes impossible to find it again! So if you want to get back there some day, you should BOOKMARK it. This is also called saving it as one of your FAVORITES, depending on what Internet program you're using.

When you're using Microsoft Internet Explorer, you can simply click on the word FAVORITES located at the top of the screen. You'll then select

ADD TO FAVORITES, and the computer will remember where that website was for you!

Q: Where is the END of the Internet?

A: The end of the Internet is at www. YouStupidComputer.biz. This is the last web site and if you go past it, you fall of the edge of the Earth.

Okay…there is no end. In fact, thousands and thousands of new web pages are added each DAY!

Q: Can I download anything I want from the Internet and use it for myself?

A: Yes—As long as you don't use it for any commercial stuff (like commercial ads). Most things that you find on the Internet are copyrighted, or at least you should assume that they are, so be careful what you do with them.

NOTES

_____

_____

_____

_____

_____

_____

_____

_____

_____

_____

_____

_____

_____

_____

_____

_____

_____

_____

_____

_____

_____

_____

_____

_____

_____

_____

_____

_____

_____

_____

_____

_____

_____

_____

_____

_____

_____

_____

_____

_____

_____

_____

_____

_____

_____

_____

_____

_____

_____

_____

_____

_____

_____

_____

_____

_____

_____

_____

_____

_____

_____

_____

_____

_____

_____

_____

_____

_____

_____

_____

_____

_____

_____

_____

_____

_____

_____

_____

_____

_____

_____

_____

_____

_____

_____

_____

_____

_____

_____

_____

_____

_____

_____

_____

VISIT US ON THE WEB

at

www.YouStupidComputer.biz

0-595-30924-0